WORLD'S FAVORITE SERIES No. 79

WORLDS

FAVORITE

PRELUDES,

OFFERTORIES,

and

POSTLUDES

for Piano

Volume II

Compiled

and Edited by

LAWRENCE GRANT

WORD

...ond volume of PRELUDES, OF-
FERTORIES, & POSTLUDES for Piano
gives the church pianist an additional selection of service music from the 17th century to the 20th century. Many of the Preludes and Offertories are suitable for either
purpose.

The cross index on Page 128 indicates
where many of the titles are in the World's
Favorite Organ albums. We hope that mu-
sicians playing in churches that use both
piano and organ will find this useful.

This volume together with World's Favor-
ite #70 PRELUDES, OFFERTORIES, &
POSTLUDES for Piano, Vol. 1, and World's
Favorite #72 WEDDING MUSIC FOR PI-
ANO provide the pianist a wide selection of
suitable music for service playing.

The Publisher

© Copyright 1973 by
ASHLEY PUBLICATIONS, INC.
263 Veterans Blvd., Carlstadt, N.J. 07072
International Copyright Secured   Made in U.S.A.

ALPHABETICAL INDEX

CLASSIFIED INDEX

CHORAL PRELUDE

JOHANNES BRAHMS, Op. 122, No. 8

PRELUDE

ALEXANDRE BOELY

Moderato

TRUMPET VOLUNTARY

JOHN BENNETT

LEGENDE

VLADIMIR REBIKOFF

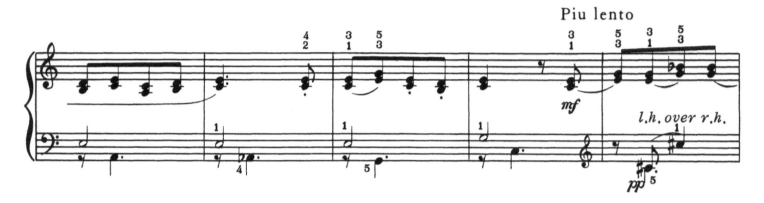

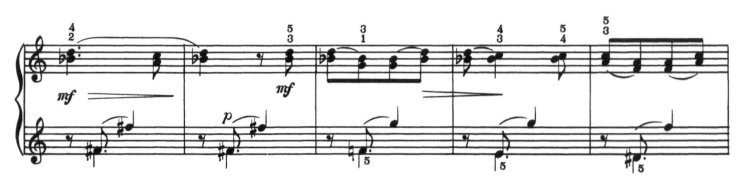

rall. poco a poco

Tempo I

pp

accel.

rallentando

INTERMEZZO
from "Cavalleria Rusticana"

PIETRO MASCAGNI
Arranged by Lawrence Grant

O HOLY NIGHT

ADOLPHE ADAM
Arranged by Lawrence Grant

STAR OF THE EAST

AMANDA KENNEDY

*r.h. chords may be rolled, if desired.

death's lone - ly night! Fear-less and tran-quil, we look up to

Thee! Know-ing thou beam'st thru e - ter - ni - ty!

Help us to fol - low where thou still dost guide, Pil-grims of

earth so wide._____ Star of the East, thou hope of the

soul, While round us here the dark bil - lows roll,

ONE SWEETLY SOLEMN THOUGHT

R. S. AMBROSE
Arranged by Lawrence Grant

Lyrics:
One sweet-ly sol - emn thought   thought   Comes to me o'er and   o'er;

I   am near-er home to-day Than I've ev - er been be - fore;

Near - er my Fa - ther's house, Where the man - y man - sions be, Near - er the great white throne,___ Near - er the crys - tal sea; Near - er the bounds of life, Where we lay our bur - dens down; Near - er leav - ing the cross,___ Near - er___ gain - ing the crown.

cresc.

pp

p

rall.

Piu mosso

But ly - ing dark-ly be - tween, _____ Wind-ing a - down thro' the

night, _____ Is the si - lent, un - known stream That

meno mosso

leads at last to the light. Fa - ther be near when my

rall.

Tranquillo

feet Are slip - ping o'er the brink, For it

may be, I am near - er home, Near - er now than I think.

dim. e rit.

AMAZING GRACE

EARLY AMERICAN MELODY
Arranged by Lawrence Grant

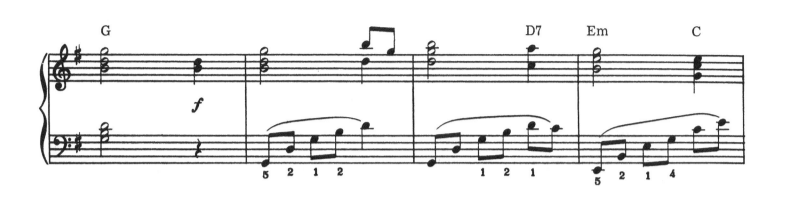

THE HOLY CITY

STEPHEN ADAMS
Arranged by Lawrence Grant

night I lay a-sleep-ing, There came a dream so fair, I stood in old Je-ru-sa-lem Be-

side the tem-ple there. I heard the chil-dren sing-ing, And ev-er as they sang, Me

thought the voice of An-gels from Heav'n in an-swer rang, Me thought the voice of

light of God was on its streets, the gates were o - pen wide, And

all who would might en - ter, And no one was de -

nied. No need of moon or stars by night, or sun to shine by

day, It was the new Je - ru - sa-lem that

would not pass a - way, It was the new Je -

NO NIGHT THERE

H. P. DANKS

Andante

In the land of fade-less day Lies the "cit-y four - square," It shall nev - er pass a - way, And there is "no night

there."   God shall   "wipe   a - way   all   tears;"   There's no

death,   no pain, nor   fears;   And they   count   not time by

years,   For there   is   "no   night   there."   *pp*

OPEN THE GATES OF THE TEMPLE

Mrs. J. F. KNAPP
Arranged by Lawrence Grant

PRELUDE AND FUGHETTA

J. O. ARMAND

PRELUDE

Andante

FUGHETTA

Allegro moderato

OH, BLEST THE HOUSE, WHATE'ER BEFALL

CHORALE MELODY
Harmonized by Johann Sebastian Bach

ETUDE IN A

DMITRI KABALEVSKY

MEDITATION

from "Thais"

JULES MASSENET
Arranged by Lawrence Grant

PRELUDE
AIR
from "Water Music in F"

GEORG FREDERIK HANDEL

PASTORALE

CHARLES WESLEY

ADAGIO

WOLFGANG A. MOZART

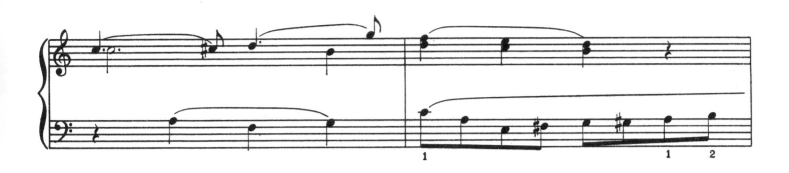

IF GOD SO CLOTHE THE GRASS

J. W. BISCHOFF
Arranged by Lawrence Grant

spin.

And yet I

say un - to you That e - ven Sol - o-mon in all his

glo - ry was not ar - ray'd like one of these.

Yet I say un - to

you That e - ven Sol-o-mon in all his glo - ry, that e - ven

dim.

f

p

p

HIS ARMS ARE OPEN TO EVERYONE

HARVEY HARDING, HAL GORDON
and JACK PERRY
Arranged by Lawrence Grant

O REST IN THE LORD

FELIX MENDELSSOHN

PRELUDE AND FUGUE

DMITRI KABALEVSKY

Andante sostenuto

A little faster

p cantando, legatissimo

*poco piu **f***

AVE MARIA

BACH-GOUNOD
Arranged by Lawrence Grant

FROM THE DEPTHS OF MY HEART

JOHANN CHRISTOPH BACH

Allegretto

IN MY DEAR GOD

DIETRICH BUXTEHUDE

Sarabande - sostenuto

with Pedal

ONLY IN THEE, LORD JESUS CHRIST

JOHANN PACHELBEL

Tranquillo

with Pedal

Offertory
COME WITH US, O BLESSED JESUS

JOHANN SCHOP
Harmonized by J. S. Bach

Cease___ not the heav'n - ly strain, But in us, Thy

lov - ing chil-dren, Bring___ peace, good will___ to men.

GLORIA PATRI

JUAN MORENO

Moderato

THE LORD IS MY SHEPHERD

SAMUEL LIDDLE

ODE TO JOY

LUDWIG van BEETHOVEN, Op. 125
Arranged by Lawrence Grant

OFFERTORY

DMITRI KABALEVSKY

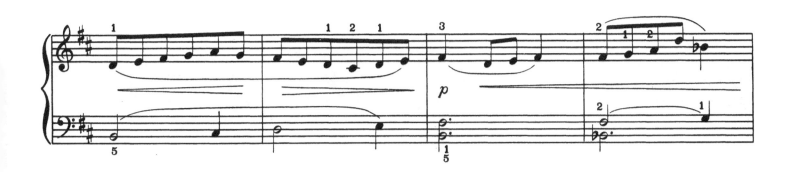

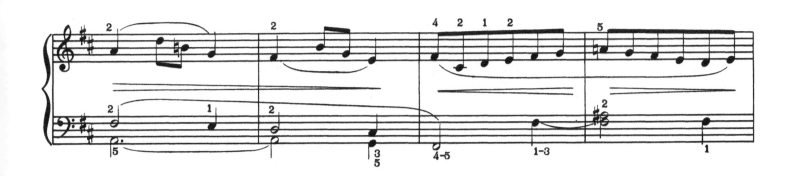

BREAK THOU THE BREAD OF LIFE

WILLIAM F. SHERWIN
Arranged by Lawrence Grant

CHORAL

BELA BARTOK

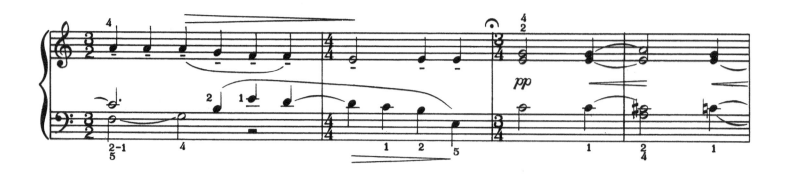

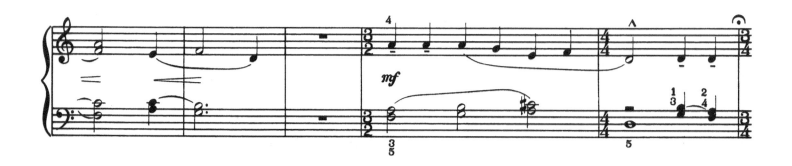

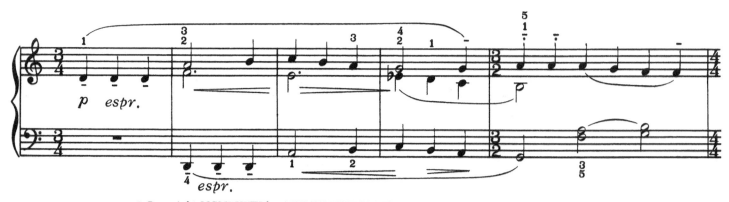

I NEED THEE EVERY HOUR

ROBERT LOWRY
Arranged by Lawrence Grant

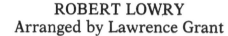
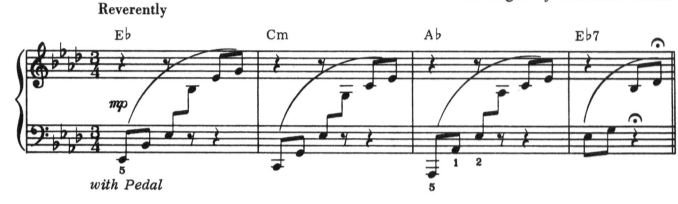
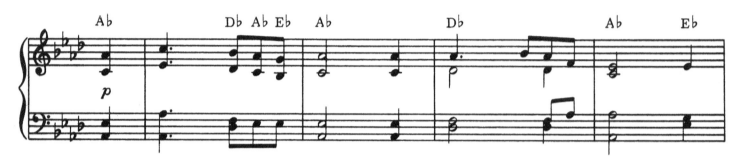
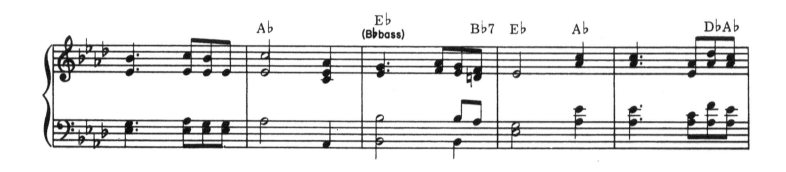

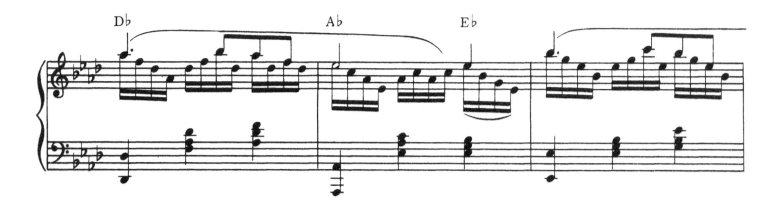

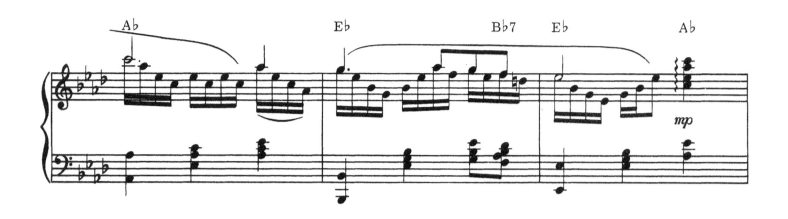

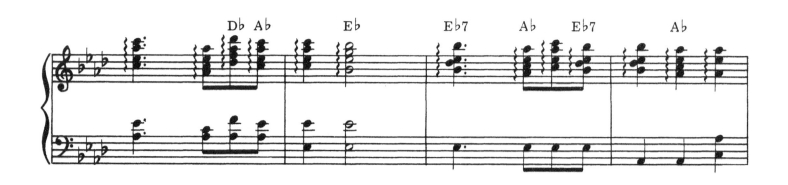

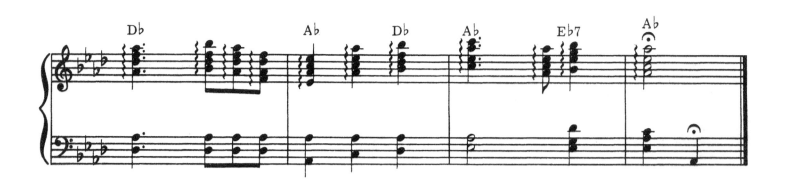

ABIDE WITH ME

WILLIAM H. MONK
Arranged by Lawrence Grant

JUST AS I AM

WILLIAM B. BRADBURY
Arranged by Lawrence Grant

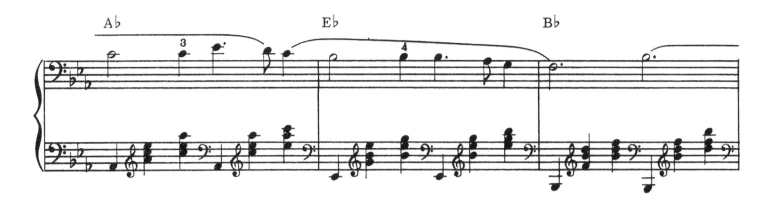

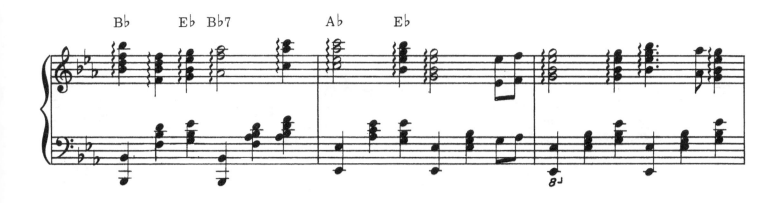

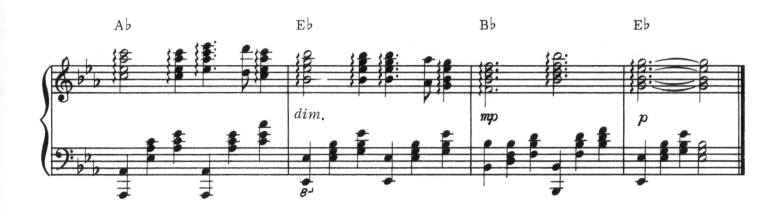

SINFONIETTA

Georg Frederic Handel

Allegro Moderato

SOFTLY AND TENDERLY

WILL L. THOMPSON
Arranged by Lawrence Grant

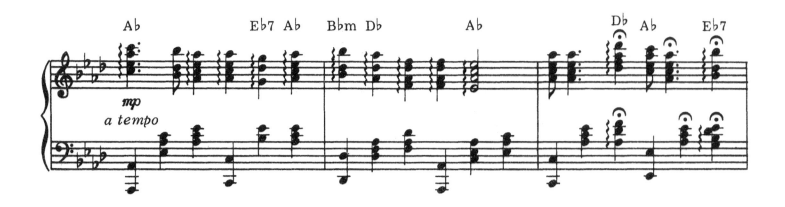

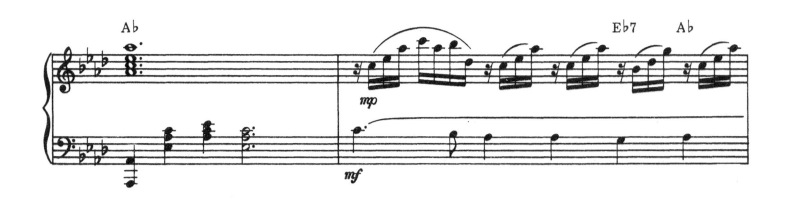

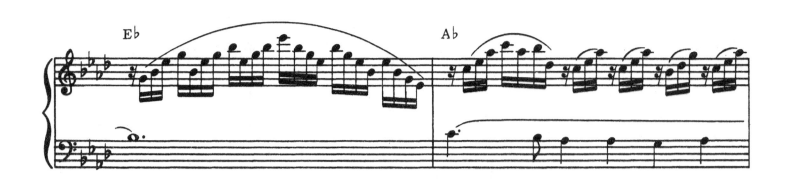

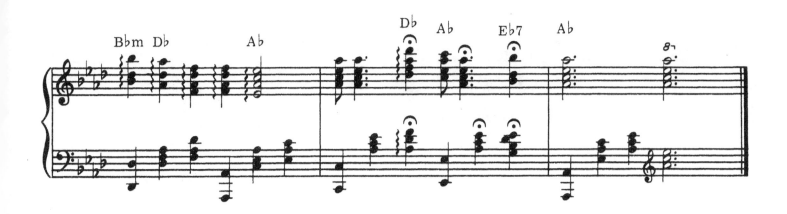

LORD BLESS YOU AND KEEP YOU

PETER C. LUTKIN
Arranged by Lawrence Grant

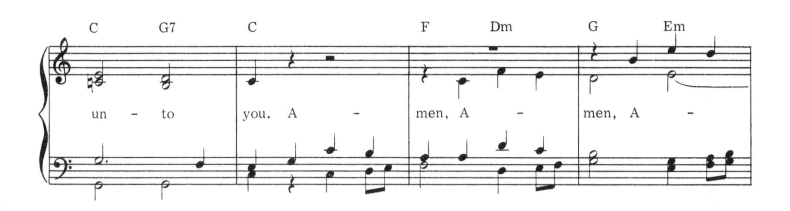

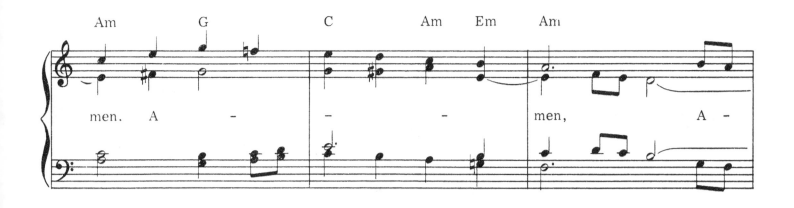

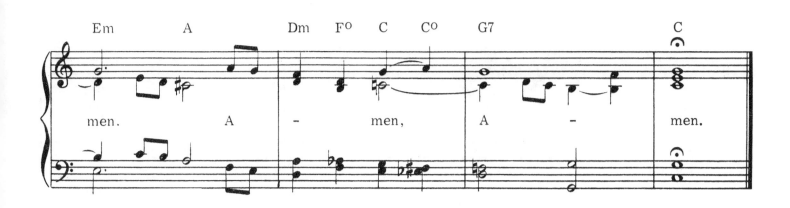

HOLD THOU MY HAND

C. S. BRIGGS
Arranged by Lawrence Grant

POSTLUDE

ALEXANDRE BOELY

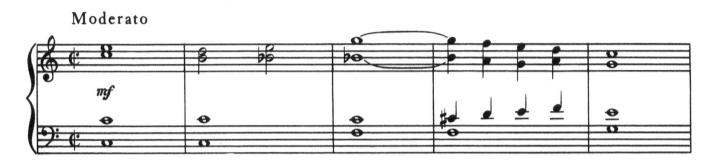

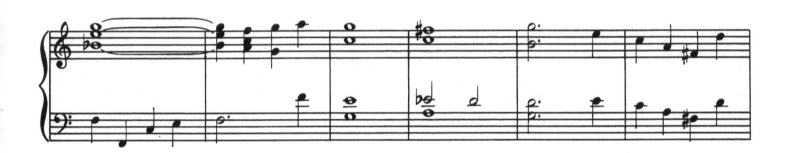

SOFTLY NOW THE LIGHT OF DAY

CARL M. VAN WEBER
Arranged by Lawrence Grant

FESTAL MARCH

J. BAPTISTE CALKIN, Op. 80

Tempo di marcia

Recessional
MARCHE ROMAINE

CHARLES GOUNOD

Allegretto maestoso

CROWN HIM WITH MANY CROWNS

GEORGE J. ELVEY
Arranged by Lawrence Grant

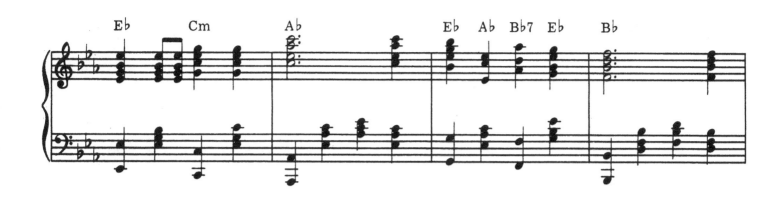

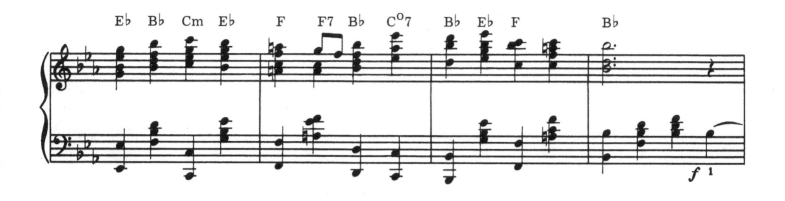

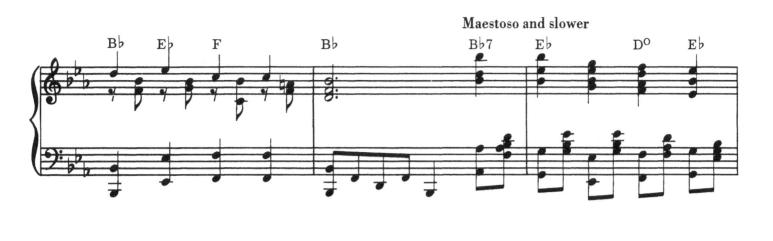

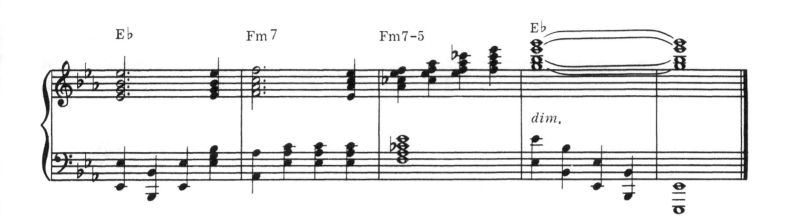

LARGO
from "The New World Symphony"

ANTONIN DVORAK, Op. 95
Arranged by Lawrence Grant

TRUMPET VOLUNTARY IN D MAJOR

HENRY PURCELL
Arranged by Lawrence Grant

ETERNAL FATHER, STRONG TO SAVE
(THE NAVY HYMN)

JOHN B. DYKES
Arranged by Lawrence Grant

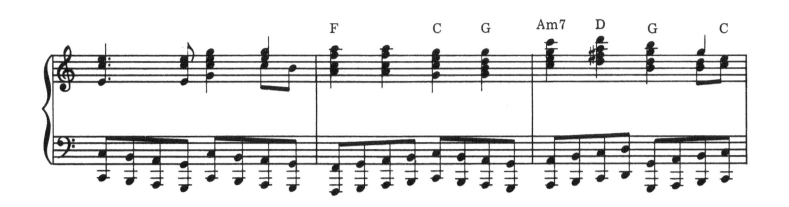

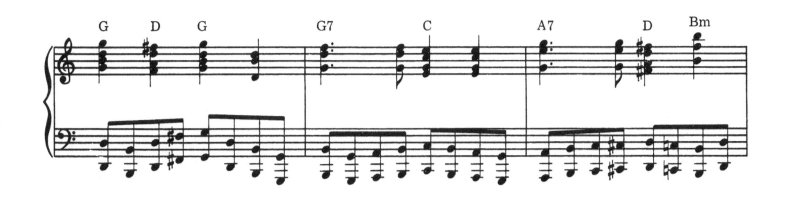

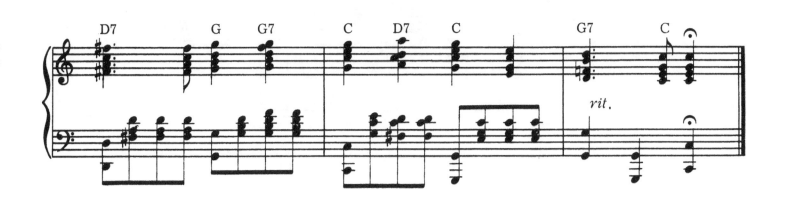

125

OUR WEDDING PRAYER

GEIGER and HATTON
Arranged by Lawrence Grant

CROSS INDEX WITH ORGAN ALBUMS

These titles from this album are also in the following organ albums. They are coordinated and may be used together when both a piano and organ are available.

KEY: WF - World's Favorite   WF53 - Hymns for All Organs
WF55 - Sacred Songs for Organ
WF58 - Wedding Music for Organ
WF59 - Easy Classics for All Organs
WF60 - Preludes, Offertories, & Postludes for Organ, Vol. 1
WF65 - Contemporary Music for Organ
WF67 - Preludes, Offertories, & Postludes for Organ, Vol. 2